AMERICA IN TROUBLE

The photograph above was taken at the National Convention of the Democratic Party of the USA, held in Chicago in June 1932. It shows a meeting of representatives of the Democratic Party from all parts of the United States. They are listening to a speech by Franklin Delano Roosevelt, a wealthy politician from New York State. He is their candidate for the Presidential election that will take place in six months' time, and he is telling them how he plans to fight the election campaign and win votes.

One sentence in Franklin D. Roosevelt's speech will help him win a landslide victory in the Presidential election. That single sentence will also make one of the most famous Presidents in American history. It is: 'I pledge you, I pledge myself, New Deal for the American people'.

The words 'New Deal' are also used by historians to sum up the long Presidency of Franklin Roosevelt, lasting from 1933 until his death in 1945. We will begin by finding out why the American people needed a 'New Deal' in the year when Roosevelt made this famous speech.

1

THE GREAT DEPRESSION

Unemployment

When Franklin D. Roosevelt made his New Deal speech in June 1932, America was in a severe economic depression. Over twelve million Americans were unemployed and the number of people out of work was going up by 12,000 every day. There was no government system of unemployment pay in America, so most people had to rely on charity to stay alive. '**Breadlines**' could be seen in every city as the unemployed lined up in queues, waiting for free bread and soup provided by charity organisations such as the Salvation Army.

Homelessness

Over a million of the unemployed were homeless. Without wages, many people could not afford to pay rent or mortgages. In 1932 alone, 250,000 Americans stopped paying their mortgages. When this happened they were evicted – thrown out – from their homes. Many took to the roads and became 'hobos', or tramps. Others moved on to waste ground in the cities where they built huts with old wood, scrap metal and sacking, which they found on rubbish dumps. They called these untidy, unhealthy camps '**Hoovervilles**' after Herbert Hoover, the President at that time.

Farmers in the countryside were just as badly off. With so many people out of work, the cities could

A 'breadline' outside the Municipal Lodging House, Christmas Day, 1932. More than 10,000 jobless and homeless men queued up for a free Christmas dinner provided by the city authorities

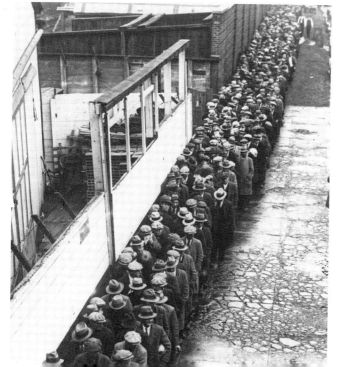

A Hooverville in New York, 1932. Note the flag on top of the pole

not afford to buy all the food the farmers produced. Farmers' incomes therefore dropped. By 1932, one in twenty of all farm-owners had been evicted from their farms because they could not afford their mortgage repayments.

Bank failures

In the Depression, many people with savings in the bank stayed alive by taking out their savings. But this led to a new problem. Some small banks did not have enough ready cash to pay savers their money, so the banks went bankrupt. When a bank failed, savers with deposits in other banks rushed to take their money out, thinking it would be safer to keep it at home. With crowds of panic-stricken savers all demanding their money at once, these banks too found that they did not have enough ready cash. Then they also had to close down. In 1932, 1616 banks had closed down for this reason, and the number of bank failures was increasing each month.

Protest

Many people affected by the Depression organised protests, hoping to improve their conditions. In the farming state of Iowa, the Farmers Union organised strikes to stop food from reaching the markets. Their aim was to create food shortages in the nearby towns, hoping that this would make food prices rise. If food prices rose, the farmers' incomes would rise too. So they blocked roads with chains and logs and they smashed the windscreens of any trucks they caught being driven to market.

Police and veterans of the 'Bonus Army' fight in the Hooverville set up by the veterans, Washington, summer 1932

The farmers also banded together to stop the eviction of farm-owners who could not pay their mortgages. Using shotguns and pitchforks, they chased away officials who tried to sell farms after evicting the owners.

The Bonus Army

The biggest protest made in 1932 was by ex-servicemen of the American army. Veteran soldiers who had fought in the Great War of 1914–18 had been promised by the government that they would be given bonus payments in 1945. But by 1932 many of the veterans were living in terrible poverty, so they demanded their bonuses now.

During the summer of 1932 veterans from all parts of the country made their way to Washington, the American capital, to protest. Many of them hijacked trains to get there and fought battles with the police who tried to stop them. By June 1932 more than 20,000 veterans had arrived in Washington and had set up a Hooverville opposite the White House, the home of the American President.

Congress, the American parliament, voted against paying the veterans their bonuses. But the '**Bonus Army**', as the veterans now called themselves, stayed in Washington to continue their protest. President Hoover ordered the army to evict them from their Hooverville. Led by General Douglas MacArthur, four companies of infantry, four troops of cavalry, a machine-gun squadron and six tanks were called out. Firing tear-gas grenades as they went, MacArthur's soldiers cleared the veterans out of the Hooverville and set it on fire. When it was all over, two veterans lay dead and 1000 were injured by tear gas.

As smoke from the burning Hooverville drifted over Washington, it seemed to many people that America was near to revolution.

Work section

A. Test your understanding of this chapter by explaining the following terms: Depression; breadline; Hooverville; bank failure; Bonus Army.

B. Read the following reports which appeared in Britain in *The Times* newspaper in 1932. Then, using the information you have read in this chapter, answer the questions beneath.

> '*Monday 30 May 1932*. The police had to be called out at New Orleans last night to force a passage out of the city for the north-bound freight train and to prevent its seizure by veterans. Tear gas had to be sprayed to keep the veterans off the train, which finally moved out of the station with forty armed policemen on the steps of the wagons.
> *Thursday 2 June 1932*. At Fort Worth last night veterans forcibly boarded a freight train to take them to Washington. Three hundred more are leaving from Oklahoma City today.
> *Tuesday 6 June*. 30,000 Bonus men in Washington. The *New York Evening Post*, in a leading article this afternoon, described it as "easily the most threatening situation the Depression has brought upon America". More than 1000 are mobilising in Los Angeles today while others from southern California are already half way across the desert in a commandeered freight train.'

1. Who were the 'veterans' mentioned in these reports? Why were they seizing trains?
2. How can you tell from these reports that the protest movement of the veterans was a nationwide movement?
3. Why do you think the *New York Evening Post* described these events as 'the most threatening situation the Depression has brought upon America'?
4. What other 'threatening situations' did the Depression cause in 1932?

2

FDR AND HH:
THE ELECTION OF 1932

Roosevelt campaigning for votes among the miners of West Virginia, 19 October 1932

Every four years, in November, elections are held for the post of President of the USA. There were two main candidates in the 1932 election. One was Herbert Hoover, who was already President and was now hoping to be re-elected for a second term of office. He represented the Republican Party, the GOP or 'Grand Old Party' as its supporters called it. The Democratic Party candidate was, as you know, Franklin Roosevelt, Governor of New York State. What were the two candidates like, and what were their ideas for dealing with the Depression?

Herbert Clark Hoover

Born in 1874, Herbert Hoover was orphaned at the age of eight. He was brought up by two uncles, working for one of them as an office boy after leaving school.

At the age of eighteen, Hoover went to university to study mine engineering. After graduating from university he worked as a gold miner, earning $2 a day for a ten-hour night shift, seven days a week.

Gradually he saved money and gained promotion to the job of assistant mining engineer. Then at the age of twenty-five he left America to work in the gold mines of Australia.

For the next fifteen years Hoover travelled the world working as a mining engineer in dozens of countries. By the age of forty he was a multi-millionaire and was able to retire from engineering in order to take up politics.

Hoover's main political belief was that the American government should not interfere in people's lives. He said that America had become rich because the people had worked hard and made money through their own individual efforts. He called this 'the American system of rugged individualism'.

In 1928 Hoover stood for election as President and won easily. At that time America was the richest country in the world. Most Americans had jobs and many were rich enough to buy luxuries such as radios, cars and refrigerators. Hoover believed that all Americans would soon be rich enough to own luxuries. He said that the time would soon come when there were 'two cars in every garage and a chicken in every pot'.

When the Depression hit America in 1929, Hoover thought it would last only a few months. Then life would return to normal. 'Prosperity is just around the corner', he said to a group of businessmen. For this reason he did not take action to end the Depression until 1932, when it was obvious that prosperity would not return by itself. He set up a **Reconstruction Finance Corporation** whose job was to lend money to companies with financial problems, in order to stop them closing down. He also made small loans to farmers and created some new jobs in a road-building programme.

Hoover's policies for dealing with the Depression came too late. When the American people went to the polls in November 1932, a huge majority decided that they did not want Hoover to be President for a second term. Although they were not sure that Roosevelt could do better, they voted for him in order to defeat Hoover. Roosevelt won the election by the biggest majority for over ninety years.

Franklin Delano Roosevelt

Born in 1882, Franklin Roosevelt came from a rich family. An only child who was pampered by his mother, Roosevelt was educated at home by private tutors until he was fourteen. Then he went to a famous public school called Groton, and after that to Harvard, America's top university.

After finishing his studies in history and law, Roosevelt decided to enter politics. He became a Senator in 1910. During the Great War of 1914–18 he had an important post in the government, helping to run the American navy. After the war, in 1920, he stood for election as Vice-President in the elections of that year. Although he lost the election, he had made a name for himself and seemed to have a promising political future ahead of him.

In 1921 Roosevelt's political career was shattered when he caught a terrible disease, polio. There was no cure for polio then, and it almost killed him. When he regained consciousness he was paralysed from the waist down.

Roosevelt spent the next five years of his life fighting against paralysis. 'I spent two years in bed trying to move my big toe', he later wrote. Gradually he learned to sit up in bed. Then, with metal struts attached to his legs, he managed to walk short distances on crutches. By 1928 Roosevelt had recovered enough to go back to politics. He stood for election for the important post of Governor of New York State, and won.

While he was Governor of New York State Roosevelt believed his main task was to make life better for ordinary people. He worked to provide old age pensions, help for farmers, and some unemployment relief. When the Depression began to affect New York State, Roosevelt spent $20 million of tax money on helping the unemployed. He was the first Governor in any state to use tax money in this way.

In 1932 Roosevelt summed up his beliefs when he said in a radio broadcast 'These unhappy times call for the building of plans . . . that put their faith once more in the forgotten man at the bottom of the economic pyramid'. It was America's 'forgotten' people – the unemployed, the homeless and hungry – who voted Roosevelt into office in the election of 1932.

Work section

A. Study this cartoon which appeared in an American newspaper on 3 March 1933. Then, using the information you have read in this chapter, answer the following questions.
 1. Who do the figures HH and FDR in the cartoon represent?
 2. What do you think the building in the background is meant to be, and why is HH leaving it?
 3. FDR is throwing out rubbish that HH has left behind. Explain what each of these pieces of rubbish means; 'chicken pot', 'car in every garage', 'prosperity is around the corner', 'rugged individualism', 'GOP policies'.
 4. What, in your opinion, was the message the cartoonist was trying to put across?

B. 1. Can you think of anything in Herbert Hoover's early life that might have led him to believe in 'rugged individualism'?
 2. Can you think of anything in Roosevelt's early life that might have led him to believe in helping the 'forgotten man'?

3

THE LAME DUCK MONTHS

A run on a bank, New York, March 1933. Panicky savers are queuing up to take their money out of the bank, but they are too late. The bank has closed its doors and stopped doing business because it has no cash left

Although Roosevelt won the Presidential election in November 1932, he could not become President until March 1933. The American constitution said that a newly elected President must wait four months until 4 March the following year before taking office. The aim of this rule was to give a new President time to prepare for his new job, and time for the retiring President to complete his work. So for four months after the election, Herbert Hoover continued to govern America, even though the electors had voted against him. These months are known as the '**lame duck**' period of a Presidency.

The lame duck months, November 1932–March 1933

Hoover spent his four lame duck months working harder than ever before. He could now see that the Depression would not go away by itself, and that he would have to take strong action. So in December 1932 Hoover announced that he would cut taxes. He would cut government spending by $800 million. He would reorganise the country's banking system. He would cut spending on weapons. Meanwhile, the Reconstruction Finance Corporation continued to give loans to companies in financial difficulty.

Roosevelt was worried by these 'lame duck' policies. He accused Hoover of 'reckless and extravagant spending'. His deputy, John Nance Garner, said that Hoover was 'leading the country down the road to socialism'.

Hoover's lame duck policies failed, however. During those four months the Depression grew worse. Unemployment rose to fifteen million. Millions of people who did have jobs found their wages being cut, and strikes began in many places. In some cities the buses and trains stopped running as transport companies went out of business. Gas and electricity were cut off as power companies went bankrupt.

6

There was worse to come. All over the country, in February 1933, banks started closing their doors for good. So many people were taking out savings from their bank accounts that the banks did not have enough ready cash to pay them. And every time that happened, panic spread as savers in nearby banks rushed to get their money out before the same happened to them.

By the start of March 1933 every bank in America was closed. People talked about a complete collapse of the American economy. And when they realised what that would mean, fear and panic spread.

'Action and action now'

On Saturday 4 March, 1933, Hoover's lame duck months came to an end. Franklin Delano Roosevelt was inaugurated, or sworn in, as thirty-second President of the United States of America. In his inaugural speech that day he said

A. 'Let me first of all assert my firm belief that the only thing we have to fear is fear itself.'

He went on to say

B. 'This nation asks for action, and action now. Our greatest primary task is to put people to work. I shall ask Congress for broad executive power [*the power to act without asking Congress for its consent*] to wage war against the emergency, as great as the power that would be given me if we were in fact invaded by a foreign foe.'

The last time America had gone to war with a 'foreign foe' had been in 1917, during the Great War. At that time, Congress passed an act which allowed President Wilson to change the law without asking Congress for its consent. The aim of this act, the **Trading with the Enemy Act**, was to allow the President to act quickly and effectively in an emergency.

The Trading with the Enemy Act was not cancelled at the end of the Great War, so it was still effective when Roosevelt became President, even though it had not been used since 1918. Roosevelt decided that America was now in a state of emergency and that he would use the Trading with the Enemy Act to deal with it. Two days after his inauguration, on 6 March, he ordered all the banks to stay closed for a long bank holiday while he and his cabinet worked out a plan for helping them to stay in business. He also forbade Americans to take gold or silver or coins of any kind out of the country.

Many Americans were glad to see that Roosevelt was dealing firmly with the crisis. But just as many were horrified. They said he was acting like a dictator, that he was ignoring the Congress, and that he was leading the country down the road to socialism.

Work section

A. Test your understanding of this chapter by explaining the following terms: lame duck period; inauguration; executive power; the Trading with the Enemy Act.

B. Study this newspaper headline which appeared on 5 March 1933 in the *New York Sunday Mirror*. Then, using the information you have read in this chapter, answer the following questions.
1. What event, the day before this newspaper appeared, do you think this headline was about?
2. At this event, what did Roosevelt say he would ask Congress for? (Read extract B from his speech above.)
3. Do you think the newspaper was fair to say 'Roosevelt asks dictator's role' about this speech? Explain your answer.
4. What did Roosevelt do on the day after this newspaper appeared to make people fear he would act like a dictator?

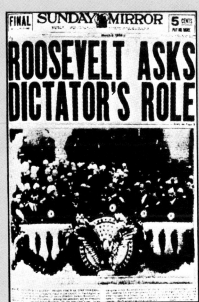

C. Study the photograph opposite. Explain why so many people were waiting outside the bank, and why it was still shut at quarter to ten in the morning.

D. Read extract A from Roosevelt's speech above.
1. What 'fear' do you think he was referring to?
2. What do you think he meant by 'The only thing we have to fear is fear itself'?

7

4

ACTION AND ACTION NOW: THE FIRST HUNDRED DAYS

Roosevelt said on 4 March 1933 'This nation asks for action, and action now'. For the next three months, the first hundred days of Roosevelt's presidency, the American people saw more action being taken to end the Depression than they had seen during the whole of Hoover's presidency.

Emergency measures

On 9 March Roosevelt called Congress together for a special meeting. He asked the members to agree to an **Emergency Banking Act**. This act said that government officials would inspect the accounts of every bank in the country. Only banks with properly managed accounts and with plenty of cash would be allowed to reopen after the bank holiday. Banks with badly managed accounts or with too little cash must stay shut.

Congress spent only half an hour discussing the Emergency Banking Act before voting unanimously for it. Three days later, on Sunday 12 March, Roosevelt spoke on the radio about the act. He said 'I can assure you that it is safer to keep your money

in a reopened bank than under the mattress'.

People listening to the President in their own homes felt as if he was with them by the fireside. They believed what he said in this 'fireside chat'. When the banks started to reopen the next morning, there was no panic. Savers did not take out their money, and in some places they started to put money back into their accounts. The banking crisis was over.

Roosevelt's next act was to cut the spending of the government. The money saved could be used to help the unemployed. On 15 March he asked Congress to vote for an **Economy Act**. This act cut the pay of everyone working in the government and the armed forces by 15 per cent. It also cut the budgets of government departments by 25 per cent. Again, Congress voted in favour, and nearly a billion dollars were saved by these measures.

Now Roosevelt began to bombard Congress with ideas for new acts. Congress passed them all. On 20 March the **Beer Act** made the manufacture and sale of beer legal again. It was the first step towards ending Prohibition, the ban on alcohol which had been imposed in 1920. It also meant that the govern-

President Roosevelt giving one of his famous 'fireside chats' on the radio in 1933. Radio broadcasting had only started in 1921, and the Presidents of the 1920s had not used the radio to speak to the people. The 'fireside chats' were therefore a great novelty for the American people

ment would make money from the tax on beer.

Now that the banking crisis was over, Roosevelt began to set up new government agencies to deal with the various problems of the Depression.

The 'alphabet agencies'

On 31 March an act of Congress set up the **Civilian Conservation Corps (CCC)**. The Cs, as people soon called it, employed young men to do conservation work in the countryside. For pocket money of a dollar a day, the young men lived in camps run by the army, doing useful conservation jobs such as tree planting, strengthening river banks, and cutting fire-breaks in forests. By August 1933 the CCC had given work to 250,000 young Americans.

To help the rest of the fifteen million unemployed, Congress agreed to set up a **Federal Emergency Relief Administration (FERA)** on 12 May. The FERA had $500 million to give to the hungry and homeless. It gave one dollar of this money to the state governments for every three dollars that they spent on helping the unemployed.

Congress passed another act on 12 May, setting up an **Agricultural Adjustment Administration (AAA)**. The aim of this agency was to help farmers increase their profits by adjusting the amount of food they grew. In many cases the AAA paid farmers to produce less, and their profits soon began to rise.

On 18 May Congress agreed to the most ambitious plan that Roosevelt had put forward so far. It was a plan for setting up a **Tennessee Valley Authority (TVA)**. The TVA was to build sixteen dams on rivers in and around the Tennessee Valley. This would provide work for thousands of construction workers and, once the dams were built, they would provide cheap hydro-electric power for industry. The dams would also help to control the frequent floods that wrecked the Tennessee Valley.

As Roosevelt's first hundred days as President came to a close, he produced two more important reforms. On 13 June Congress agreed to a **Home Owners Loan Corporation (HOLC)**. This would help home-owners keep up with their mortgage repayments by lending them money at low interest rates. Finally, on 16 June, Congress passed the National Industrial Recovery Act. This important act was in two parts, both designed to help industry recover from the Depression. One part of the act set up a **Public Works Administration (PWA)**. The job of the PWA was to create work for unemployed industrial workers by starting big work schemes of public benefit – building bridges, new houses and roads, for example. The other part of the act set up a **National Recovery Administration (NRA)**. The aim of the NRA was to persuade employers in industry to pay their workers fair wages and to charge fair prices for their goods.

On 16 June the special session of Congress that Roosevelt had called came to an end, and the 'hundred days' were over. Roosevelt's critics and opponents still grumbled that he was acting like a dictator. They made fun of the agencies he had set up, calling them 'alphabet agencies' because they were known by their initials – CCC, FERA, AAA, and so on.

But everyone admitted that things were starting to change. Walter Lippmann, a leading American journalist, wrote shortly afterwards:

> 'In the hundred days from March to June we became again an organised nation confident of our power to . . . control our own destiny.'

Roosevelt was clearly providing Americans with the New Deal he had promised in 1932. But whether or not the New Deal would work remained to be seen.

Work section

A. Test your understanding of this chapter by explaining the following terms: Congress; fireside chat; alphabet agencies; hundred days.

B. Make a time chart of the first hundred days of Roosevelt's Presidency, 4 March to 16 June 1933. Then write in the names of the emergency acts that Congress passed and the alphabet agencies it created during this time.

Example:

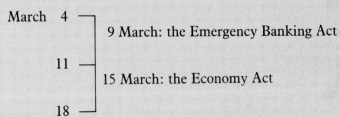

March   4

9 March: the Emergency Banking Act

11

15 March: the Economy Act

18

(Use a line 15 cm long, with 1 cm for each week.)

C. Before going any further, make revision notes on what you have read so far. There is a note guide on the next page to help you.

Revision guide

These revision notes may either be copied or used as a framework for your own notes. If you decide to copy them you will have to fill in a blank word or number in each point.

A. The Great Depression

1. In 1932 . . million Americans were out of work. Most had to live on c. . . . . . because there was no unemployment pay. In every city the unemployed queued up in b. . . . . for free food.
2. Over a million of the unemployed were homeless because they could not afford rent or mortgages. Many lived in camps made of rubbish which they called H. . . . .
3. Farmers in the countryside were very badly off. By 1932 one farmer in twenty had been e. . . . . from his farm because he could not afford the mortgage repayments.
4. During the Depression banks began to close down when too many savers tried to withdraw their savings at the same time. By 1932 1. . . banks had gone bankrupt.
5. Many people affected by the Depression joined protests against the government. Farmers in the state of I. . . organised farmers' strikes. Thousands of ex-servicemen formed a 'B. . . . A. . .' and went to Washington to demand early payment of their war bonuses. Even though the army drove them out of Washington, their action made many people fear that America was close to revolution.

B. The Presidential election of 1932

1. In the 1932 election for the Presidency, Herbert Hoover was the candidate for the R. . . . . Party, and F. . . . . . R. . . . . . . was the candidate for the Democratic Party.
2. Herbert Hoover was a mining e. . . . . . from the age of 21 and a millionaire by 40. He believed that the Depression would not last long. He also believed that the government should not interfere in people's lives; people should work hard and look after their own interests. He called this the 'American system of r. . . . . i. . . . .'. For this reason Hoover did little to fight the Depression. He set up a R. . . . . F. . . . . C. . . . . to lend money to industry, and he gave some loans to farmers. But by the time of the election these measures had not improved the situation.
3. Franklin D. Roosevelt came from a wealthy family. He entered politics after Harvard University and quickly made a name for himself. In 1921 he caught p. . . . and was never able to walk again. He became the Governor of New York State in 1928. During the Depression he spent state money on helping the unemployed. He believed the government should make plans to help the 'f. . . . . . . m. .' – i.e. the unemployed.

C. The lame duck months, 1932–3

1. Roosevelt was elected President in November 1932 but did not take office until March 1933. During these months Hoover continued as a 'lame duck' President.
2. In December 1932 Hoover took stronger action against the Depression. He cut government s. . . . . . and gave more loans to industry, but these policies did not work and unemployment rose to . . million, strikes broke out, banks failed, and the country ground to a halt.
3. When Roosevelt was sworn in as President on 4 March 1933 he said that America needed 'A. . . . and a. . . . . now'.
4. Using the powers of the Trading with the E. . . . Act, Roosevelt shut all banks for a long bank holiday while he and his advisers worked out what to do.

D. The Hundred Days, March–June 1933

During the first hundred days of Roosevelt's Presidency, a special session of Congress passed a series of acts:

1. The E. . . . . . . B. . . . . Act reopened sound banks.
2. The E. . . . . A. . cut government spending.
3. The B. . . Act made the manufacture and sale of beer legal.
4. Young unemployed men were given conservation work by the C. . . . . . . C. . . . . C. . . . .
5. The Federal Emergency Relief Administration gave money to the unemployed.
6. The A. . . . . A. . . . . A. . . . . aimed to help farmers by raising food prices.
7. The Tennessee river was to be dammed by the T. . . . . . . V. . . . A. . . . .
8. Home owners were helped by the H. . . O. . . . . L. . . C. . . . .
9. The National Industrial Recovery Act aimed to revive industry by setting up two agencies, the P. . . . . W. . . . A. . . . . and the N. . . . . . . R. . . . . . A. . . . .

PART TWO
A NEW DEAL

'Migrant mother and children', 1936. This family has moved to California in search of work and a better life

During the New Deal years, 1933 to 1939, the American government paid a group of out-of-work photographers to make a record of how the Depression affected ordinary people. Probably the most famous picture taken by the group was the one above. The photographer, Dorothea Lange, seems to have captured in one woman's face the feelings of despair that millions of Americans experienced.

President Roosevelt's New Deal was meant to help families like this one – and help them quickly. America, he said in 1933, needed 'action and action now'.

Part Two of this book shows how Roosevelt tried to carry out his promise to give the American people a New Deal. It is for you to judge whether or not he succeeded.

5

A NEW DEAL FOR THE UNEMPLOYED

You found out in Chapter 4 that Roosevelt set up two agencies to help the unemployed during his first hundred days as President. The PWA, the Public Works Administration, was to create work for the unemployed by starting public works schemes. The FERA, the Federal Emergency Relief Administration, was to give $500 million to the states for the relief of the hungry and the homeless.

Harry Hopkins and the CWA

The official in charge of the Federal Emergency Relief Administration was Harry Hopkins, a former social worker who had strong views on how to help the unemployed. The FERA should give them work, not dole money, he believed. He said that keeping workers on the dole took away their pride and destroyed their morale, whereas 'work relief preserves a man's morale. It saves his skill. It gives him a chance to do something socially useful.'

Many people disagreed with Harry Hopkins. They said that the cost of work relief was much greater than the cost of paying dole money to the unemployed. They also pointed out that the PWA had already been set up to organise work schemes. Hopkins replied that the PWA would not start providing jobs until the following year; in the meantime, with winter coming, millions of the unemployed still needed work.

Hopkins won the argument about work relief. In November 1933 Roosevelt set up a new agency and put Hopkins in charge of it. This agency was the **Civil Works Administration** (**CWA**). Within two months Hopkins and the CWA had found work for four million people, paying them 40 cents an hour for unskilled jobs and $1 an hour for skilled work.

Over the next three months CWA workers did all the following:

- built or improved 800,000 km of roads
- built or improved 40,000 schools
- built 500 airports and improved 500 more
- built 150,000 public toilets.

Not all CWA jobs had an obvious public value, however. Thousands of people were paid to sweep up leaves in their local parks. Unemployed actors were hired to give free shows. The CWA even paid out-of-work researchers to research the history of the safety pin, and hired 100 people in Washington to walk the streets with balloons to frighten pigeons away from public buildings. People soon began to call such jobs

Rival New Dealers: left, Harry Hopkins of the CWA and WPA; right, Harold Ickes of the PWA

'boondoggles', after plaits that American cowboys made from leather strips to pass the time when they had no work to do.

Harry Hopkins defended the CWA against the accusation that he was providing 'boondoggles' for the unemployed. When someone criticised him for paying out-of-work librarians to catalogue archives, he said 'Hell, they've got to eat just like other people'.

Once the winter of 1933–4 was over the CWA was disbanded and four million people again found themselves out of work.

Harold Ickes and the PWA

Meanwhile the Secretary of the Interior, Harold Ickes, was organising the **Public Works Administration** (**PWA**). Unlike Harry Hopkins, Harold Ickes was very careful with the government's money. He believed that work schemes organised by the PWA should make things of lasting use to the nation, and he hated the idea of paying workers to 'boondoggle'.

Between 1933 and 1939 the PWA did all the following:

- built 70 per cent of America's schools
- built 35 per cent of America's hospitals
- built four big river dams
- electrified the New York-Washington railway
- built two aircraft carriers, four cruisers and four destroyers for the US Navy
- built 50 military airports
- built a new sewage system in Chicago.

Nobody accused Harold Ickes and the PWA of 'boondoggling', and many people admired its achievements. But the PWA only provided work for skilled and able-bodied workers. It did nothing for the millions who lacked a skill or a trade.

Harry Hopkins and the WPA

To help the unskilled, Harry Hopkins set up a new work relief agency in 1935, the **Works Progress Administration (WPA)**. The WPA soon became the country's biggest employer, giving work to an average of two million people each year.

Between 1933 and 1939 the WPA helped to build:

- 11,000 schools
- 70,000 km of new roads
- La Guardia airport in New York.

The WPA also gave work to artists of all kinds. Unemployed writers were paid to write a series of guide books to America's states and cities. Painters made pictures for display in schools and other public buildings. Twelve thousand actors were sent on tour to perform in shows and plays across the country. Photographers such as Dorothea Lange (see page 11) were employed to make a photographic record of the Depression years.

The CWA, the PWA and the WPA provided work for millions of people. The wages they earned allowed them to buy food, clothing and other goods. As people began to buy again, farmers, shopkeepers, businessmen and factory owners began to make profits again. The more profits they made, the more they were able to expand their businesses, and that meant even more jobs for the unemployed.

Work section

A. Study this photograph taken in 1935 in the town of Schroon Lake. Then, using the information you have read in this chapter, answer the following questions:

1. Which of the 'alphabet agencies' of the New Deal organised this public work project? Who was in charge of this agency?
2. How can you tell from the photograph that thousands of public work projects were started in 1935?
3. How many companies gained work from this project? What kinds of worker do you think found work on the project?
4. Why might Harry Hopkins have criticised this project as a way of providing work for the unemployed?

B. Make a list like the one below of suggestions for work schemes for the unemployed. Tick the schemes you think Harry Hopkins might have supported, then tick the schemes you think Harold Ickes might have supported. In each case explain why. (NB Bear in mind that they might agree in some cases.)

	Harry Hopkins	Harold Ickes
1. Build a 500 km, six lane highway linking Los Angeles with San Francisco. 50,000 men needed for two years.		
2. Build a dam for hydro-electric power on the Snake River in Idaho. 4000 men needed for five years.		
3. Build children's playgrounds in every precinct of Chicago. Work for 100 men for eighteen months		
4. Electrify the New York to Boston railway. Work for 200 electricians and riggers for two years.		
5. Publish a complete history of the United States of America. Work for six historians for five years.		
6. Plant 20,000 trees to beautify the streets of Washington. Work for 20 gardeners for six months.		
7. Build a new deep sea dock for US Navy battleships in Norfolk, Virginia. Work for 1000 for three years.		

C. Whose ideas for giving work to the unemployed do you most agree with – Harry Hopkins or Harold Ickes? Explain your answer.

6

A NEW DEAL FOR THE FARMERS

Families of 'Okies' – farming people who have left the Dust Bowl in Oklahoma to find work and start new lives in California, 1935

The plight of the farmers

In January 1933 Ed O'Neal, leader of a farmers' union, said

> 'Unless something is done for the American farmer we will have revolution in the countryside within less than twelve months.'

Of all the groups hit by the Great Depression, the farmers were worst off. The price of food was so low that they could not make any profit when they sold their crops at market. As a result their incomes dropped. Many farmers tried growing more crops, hoping to make a profit through bigger sales, but this simply made prices drop even lower.

By 1933 one farm-owner in twenty had been evicted from his land because he could not keep up with the mortgage repayments. In this desperate situation, many farm-owners took matters into their own hands. In April 1933 500 farmers in the state of Iowa broke into a court-house where Judge Charles Bradley was signing orders for the eviction of farmers from their land. They dragged Judge Bradley from his court-house, smeared him with tractor-grease and then tried to hang him. It seemed as if law and order were breaking down in the countryside, and the

Governor of Iowa put much of the state under martial law.

With revolution threatening to break out in the countryside, President Roosevelt made helping farmers a priority task.

Agricultural adjustment

Roosevelt instructed Henry Wallace, the Secretary of Agriculture, to make plans for immediate aid to farmers. On 12 May 1933 the **Agricultural Adjustment Administration** (**AAA**) came into being. Henry Wallace's aim in setting up the AAA was to reduce the size of farmers' crops by 'adjusting' them. His idea was that if smaller amounts of farm produce were sold at market, the price would rise, giving the farmers bigger profits.

The AAA set to work immediately – by giving farmers money to destroy their crops! Many thousands of cotton farmers received over $100 million for ploughing that summer's cotton crop into the ground.

Many Americans were horrified by this policy of the AAA. They were even more angry when the AAA bought six million baby pigs from hog farmers and slaughtered them all. Even though the meat was canned and given away free to the unemployed, it seemed crazy for the government to pay farmers not to produce food.

Despite all the objections the AAA's adjustment of farm prices worked. Prices quickly rose, and with them rose farmers' incomes.

The problem of the sharecroppers

The AAA policy of crop adjustment helped farmers who owned their own land, but it did nothing for the people who worked for them – the sharecroppers.

Over half the three million sharecroppers in America were black, and most lived in slum conditions. Erskine Caldwell, an American writer, visited a two-room shack shared by three families of sharecroppers in 1933. This is what he saw:

> 'In one of the two rooms a six-year old boy licked the paper bag the meat had been brought in. His legs were scarcely any larger than a medium-sized dog's legs, and his belly was as large as that of a 130 pound [59 kg] woman's . . . . On the floor beside an open fire lay two babies, neither a year old, sucking the dry teats of a mongrel bitch.'

The AAA policy of destroying crops made conditions even worse for the sharecroppers. Once they had helped the farm-owner destroy the year's crop, there was no work left for them to do, and no crop for them to share. Thousands had to pack their belongings and leave their slum homes to look for work in other parts of the country.

The Dust Bowl

On the high plains of the Midwest, a new crisis in American agriculture began in 1934, ruining farm-owners as well as sharecroppers.

The summer of 1934 was very hot and dry. The blazing sun scorched the earth and turned much of

The Dust Bowl: the scene on a farm in South Dakota after a dust storm in May 1936

the land in the Midwest into a huge 'Dust Bowl' of loose, dry earth. In the autumn strong winds blew away the earth in massive dust storms that made normal life impossible. Schools and factories had to shut down when the wind blew. Street lights shone during the day as dust clouds blotted out the sun. Cars and lorries were buried in great drifts of choking dirt.

The effect of these 'black blizzards' on farms in the Dust Bowl was even more serious. Tens of thousands of farms were destroyed, especially in the states of Oklahoma and Arkansas. When this happened, all the farmers could do was load their belongings on to a car or a truck, and move away. Throughout the 1930s over 350,000 'Okies' and 'Arkies' made their way west to the rich farming states beyond the Dust Bowl, especially to California and Oregon.

Work section

A. Read this letter written in 1935, then answer the questions beneath.
'Corn is 70 cents . . . on the farms in Iowa. Two years ago it was 10 cents. Top hogs sold in Iowa plants yesterday at $7.40, or $4.50 to $5 better than a year ago. Farmers are very happy and convinced of the virtue of planning . . . Secretary Wallace can have whatever he wants from Iowa farmers.'

Senator Louis Murphy, writing to President Roosevelt in 1935.

1. Who was 'Secretary Wallace'? What government agency did he set up in 1933?
2. By how much did the price of corn increase between 1933 and 1935 according to Senator Murphy? What do you think caused its price to rise?
3. By how much did the price of 'hogs' increase between 1934 and 1935 according to Senator Murphy? How did the government bring about an increase in pig prices?
4. Judging by what you have read in this chapter, why do you think it is surprising that farmers in the state of Iowa were 'very happy'?

B. Carefully study the two photographs in this chapter. In each case explain what caused the situation you see in the photograph.

A NEW DEAL FOR THE LAND

Badly eroded land in the Tennessee Valley, 1930

Two of the most famous 'alphabet agencies' of the New Deal did more than give jobs to the unemployed. They also improved the quality of the environment. The results of their work can still be seen today.

The Three Cs

President Roosevelt was born and brought up in the countryside, and he was an expert on the subject of conserving the land. His favourite agency for helping the unemployed therefore aimed also to improve the environment in the American countryside. This was the **Civilian Conservation Corps (CCC)** which Roosevelt set up in March 1933, the first of all the 'alphabet agencies'.

The CCC gave work to unmarried men aged 18 to 25 whose parents were out of work. It was run jointly by the US Army and the US Forestry Service which set up work camps in America's woods and forests. By July 1933, 300,000 young men were living in 13,000 camps all over America. By 1938 some two million had served in the CCC, most of them for periods of six months to a year.

The men in the CCC camps were given food, clothing and shelter – either in huts or tents – in return for their work. They also got pocket money of one dollar a day, but camp rules said that they had to send $25 home to their parents each month.

The CCC worked mainly to improve and conserve the country's forests. In the Midwest it planted more than 200 million trees in a 17 million acre 'shelter-belt' to stop soil erosion. Over half the trees growing in America today were planted by the CCC during the New Deal years.

As well as planting trees the CCC did all the following:

- made reservoirs and fish ponds
- built fire look-out posts in forests
- treated tree diseases like Dutch Elm disease
- cleared up beaches and camping grounds
- restored historic battlefields.

Lunch time at a CCC camp in Tennessee, November 1933

President Roosevelt said in 1934 'The CCC activity has probably been the most successful of anything we have done. There is not a word of complaint – rap on wood.' A survey of CCC members four years later seemed to confirm this:

'I weighed about 160 pounds [*73 kg*] when I went there, and when I left I was 190 [*86 kg*] about. It made a man out of me all right.

'Here they teach you how to pour concrete and lay stones and drive trucks, and if a boy wants to go and get a job after he's been in the "Cs" he'll know how to work.'

'It helps you to get along with other people in general, because it helps you to get over being selfish.'

The TVA

America's biggest environmental problem when Roosevelt became President was in the Tennessee Valley (see map opposite). The Tennessee at that time was a dangerous river. Every spring it flooded, washing away millions of tonnes of topsoil and destroying the farms in the area. In summer it often dried to a trickle, parching the farmlands. Each year the eroded land of the Tennessee Valley produced fewer and fewer crops. The people living there grew poorer and hungrier until, by 1933, half were living on dole money paid by the state. The Tennessee Valley, an area as large as England and Wales put together, had become what Roosevelt called 'the nation's number one economic problem'.

It was a problem far too big for the CCC to handle, so in May 1933 Roosevelt set up a **Tennessee Valley Authority** (**TVA**) to tackle it.

The TVA began by building dams on the Tennessee river and its tributaries. At the touch of a button the dam controllers could close massive sluice-gates to hold back the river when it threatened to flood. In all, the TVA built twenty-one massive dams over the next ten years.

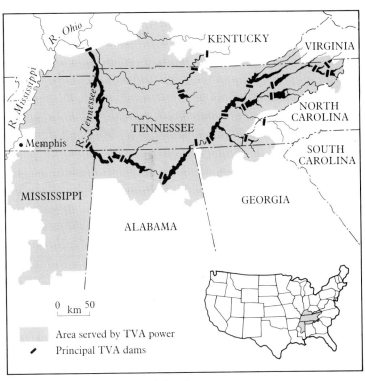

The Tennessee Valley and its dams

The TVA dams brought many benefits to the region. First, they were used to make cheap electricity. Powerful turbines built into the walls of the dams were driven by jets of water released from the lakes behind them. By 1940 the twenty-one dams were producing 3.2 billion kilowatts of electricity each year.

A second benefit of the dams came from the lakes that built up behind them. The lakes were long, wide and deep – ideal for water transport. Locks built into the sides of the dams meant that ships could now travel 1000 km up the river, carrying coal, steel and other products to the region's factories. The factories could also now transport their products to distant areas for sale, and this increased their profits.

Gradually the poverty of the Tennessee Valley disappeared. By 1940 it was a prosperous area, the pride of Roosevelt's New Deal.

Work section

A. Study the statements above by three members of the CCC, then answer these questions:
1. What advantages, according to these statements, were there in working for the CCC?
2. Judging by what you have read in this chapter, can you think of any disadvantages of working in the CCC? Think particularly about how long CCC jobs lasted for, about the pay, and about where the work camps were.
3. In your opinion, were the advantages of working in the CCC greater than or less than the disadvantages? Explain your answer.

B. Study the photograph opposite of eroded land in the Tennessee Valley. Using the information you have read in this chapter, explain how this land came to be eroded.

C. Study the map above, then answer these questions:
1. How many states were affected by the work of the Tennessee Valley Authority?
2. How many dams did the TVA build, and on how many rivers were they built?
3. List three ways in which the TVA dams helped to improve the Tennessee Valley.

8

A NEW DEAL FOR INDUSTRY

Industry was the heart of the American economy. The profits from steel, textiles, cars, oil, timber, and a thousand other products, had made America the world's leading industrial nation. In 1933, however, the industrial heart of the economy was beating faintly and threatening to stop completely.

The problems of industry

During the Great Depression the demand for goods dropped sharply. This meant that factory owners had to cut down the amount of goods they produced, and that in turn meant sacking workers. So profits for factory owners fell while unemployment rose.

In an effort to sell more goods, many factory owners cut their prices. Often they reduced their prices so much that they could only make profits by cutting their workers' wages and making them work longer hours. In many cases they used cheap, or 'sweated' labour. In the state of Connecticut an official enquiry in 1932 recorded the following:

A. '. . . the existence of over a hundred sweatshops hiring young girls for as little as 60¢ to $1.10 for a 55 hour week. A family of six, including four children, were found stringing safety pins on wires late into the night for 4 to 5 dollars a week.'

Workers sometimes tried to improve their pay and conditions by forming trade unions. But the factory owners went to amazing lengths to stop them: they feared that trade unions would force them to pay higher wages to their workers. Henry Ford, the car manufacturer, used strong-arm men to deal with unionists in his factories, as this extract shows:

B. 'There are about 800 underworld characters in the Ford organisation. They are the storm troops. They make no pretence of working, but are merely 'keeping order' through terror. Around this nucleus of 800 yeggs [*gangsters*] there are between 8000 and 9000 spies and stool-pigeons [*informers*]. Because of this highly organised terror and spy system the fear in the plant is something indescribable. During the lunch hour the men shout at the top of their voices about the baseball scores lest they be suspected of talking unionism. Workers seen talking together are taken off the assembly line and fired. Every man suspected of union sympathies is immediately dismissed, usually under the framed-up charge of "starting a fight" in which he often gets terribly beaten up.'

The NRA and the Blue Eagle

To revive the fluttering heart of American industry, Roosevelt put forward the **National Industrial Recovery Act** in June 1933. One part of the act set up the PWA which, as you have read (Chapter 5) created jobs for the unemployed on public work schemes. The other part of the act created a **National Recovery Administration** (**NRA**). Roosevelt said in a speech that the aim of the NRA was 'the assurance of a reasonable profit to industry and living wages to labour'. In other words, factories should try to make profits, but without using sweated or child labour.

The official in charge of the NRA was General Hugh Johnson, a hard-drinking, hard-working and bad-tempered ex-soldier who had helped run American industry during the Great War. Johnson drew up codes of fair competition which he asked factory owners and businessmen to sign. These codes fixed fair prices for the goods they were selling and laid down minimum wages and conditions of work for their employees. For example, the Cotton Textile code fixed a 40 hour week, abolished child labour under the age of 16, provided a minimum wage of $12 in the southern states and $13 in the north, and allowed cotton workers to join trade unions.

When a company signed a NRA code it was allowed to use the symbol of the NRA to help advertise its products. The symbol was a blue eagle

'Miss Liberty' and 'Miss NRA' lead a procession down Fifth Avenue, New York, during the NRA parade in September 1933

clutching a cogwheel and a sheaf of thunderbolts in its talons. With the blue eagle went the motto 'We Do Our Part'.

By September 1933 over 500 industries, ranging from boilermaking to laundering, had signed NRA codes. They covered 2 million employers and 22 million workers. In New York a massive parade was held to celebrate the NRA. More than 250,000 marchers poured down Fifth Avenue singing 'Happy Days Are Here Again'.

Problems

Unfortunately the NRA quickly ran into difficulties. Employers who hated trade unions – Henry Ford, for example – refused to sign the codes because they wanted to prevent their workers from unionising. Others signed the codes but then ignored the parts of the codes they did not like.

When workers found out that their employers were anti-trade union, they often lost their enthusiasm for the NRA and went on strike. By September 1933 nearly 300,000 workers were on strike, and the number was increasing rapidly every month.

Meanwhile, complaints about the codes were being made by companies which had signed them, particularly by small laundries which had signed the Cleaners and Dyers code. The small laundries were in cut-throat competition with each other, and they often accused each other of breaking the code on minimum wages. When the NRA took legal action against the laundries that broke the code, the laundries complained that the government was bullying small businessmen trying to make an honest living. But if the NRA took no action, the other companies complained that the codes meant nothing since their rivals could get away with breaking them.

Within a year of being created, it seemed that the 'happy days' were still a long way off in industry. The NRA was upsetting both the workers, whom it aimed to protect, and the businessmen, whom it aimed to encourage.

9

OPPOSITION TO THE NEW DEAL

The Supreme Court and the 'Sick Chickens' case

In Brooklyn, a borough of New York City, four brothers called Schechter ran a small but profitable poultry business, the Schechter Poultry Corporation. In 1933, along with other poultry firms in New York, they signed a NRA code agreeing to the NRA rules of fair prices, fair wages and fair competition.

In 1935 the Schechter brothers broke one of the NRA codes by selling a batch of diseased chickens that were not fit for human consumption. The NRA took the Schechters to court. When the brothers were found guilty by the court of breaking a NRA code, they appealed against the verdict. Their appeal was heard by the Supreme Court, America's highest court, consisting of nine judges.

The Supreme Court declared that the NRA had no right to meddle in the New York poultry trade. The nine judges said it was a matter for the New York State government to investigate, not the federal government in Washington. The Schechter brothers were acquitted and the code they had signed was declared illegal.

The case of the 'sick chickens' destroyed the NRA. When the supreme court declared that the poultry code was illegal, all similar codes automatically became illegal. Overnight the NRA had to scrap 750 of its codes.

More problems for the New Deal agencies lay ahead in the Supreme Court. In 1936 the Court declared that the AAA, the Agricultural Adjustment Administration, went against the constitution and was therefore illegal. The nine judges said that giving help to farmers was a matter for each state government, not the federal government. Thus all the help that the AAA gave to farmers suddenly stopped.

In all, the Supreme Court tried sixteen cases concerning the 'alphabet agencies' of the New Deal. In eleven of these cases the judges declared that President Roosevelt and Congress had acted against the country's constitution. They said that Roosevelt had misused the power of the federal government; the federal government, they declared, was responsible only for national affairs affecting all the states. The state governments were responsible for all other affairs.

A. *A cartoon from the Chicago newspaper* Tribune *in September 1935 on the quarrel between Roosevelt and the Supreme Court*

B. *A British cartoon from* Punch *in June 1935 on the quarrel between Roosevelt and the Supreme Court*

Roosevelt was furious about the Supreme Court's decisions. His view was that the alphabet agencies *were* dealing with matters of national concern. He said that the Great Depression affected the whole country, not just individual states. But the Court would not change its mind, so Roosevelt was powerless to stop the nine judges from wrecking his New Deal programme.

Other ideas for a New Deal

While the Supreme Court was busy attacking the legality of the New Deal, a number of ambitious politicians were criticising it for not doing enough to solve America's problems.

Senator **Huey Long** from the state of Louisiana was the best known opponent of the New Deal. Huey Long started his political career in 1928 when he became Governor of Louisiana. When the Depression hit Louisiana he did all he could to help the poor – by spending public money on building roads and new hospitals, and by providing free school books. His slogan was 'Every man a king, but no man wears a crown'. Many people disagreed with Huey Long's extreme ideas, but he kept a gang of strong-arm men to deal with anyone who disagreed too loudly.

In 1932 Huey Long became Senator for Louisiana. In speeches in the Senate he criticised Roosevelt for doing too little to help the poor. He put forward an alternative to the New Deal called the '**Share Our Wealth**' movement. He promised that, if he was President, all fortunes of over $3 million would be confiscated. The money would be used to give every American family a sum of $4000 to $5000 to buy a home, a car and a radio. There would be free education for all Americans, a national minimum wage, old age pensions, houses for war veterans and cheap food for the poor.

In Louisiana the 'Kingfish', as Huey Long was known, put many of his ideas into practice. But he also used his power as Governor to get rid of opponents, to rig local elections, and to bribe the police. By 1935 he was virtually a dictator, running Louisiana in exactly the way he wanted.

His great power, however, could not stop a doctor, whose family he had ruined, from pulling a gun on him outside his office in New Orleans. Although Long's bodyguards pumped sixty-one bullets into the doctor before he could fire a single shot, a single bullet ricocheting from the corridor wall entered Long's stomach and killed him.

Another ambitious opponent of the New Deal was **Father Charles Coughlin**, a Roman Catholic priest. Often called 'the radio priest', because he ran a popular weekly radio programme, Coughlin set up the '**National Union for Social Justice**' in 1935. Its main aim was to provide work and fair wages for everyone.

Coughlin claimed that Roosevelt was 'anti-God' and decided to fight him in the Presidential elections due in 1936. To improve his chances in the election, Coughlin joined forces with another opponent of the New Deal, **Frances Townsend**, a retired doctor from California. In California, nearly 10 per cent of the population was aged sixty-five or over. In the Depression old people could be seen scrounging in dustbins for food scraps. Doctor Townsend wanted the federal government to give $200 a month to every citizen over the age of sixty. The money for this would come from a 2 per cent sales tax.

Townsend and Coughlin had millions of supporters. When the two of them joined forces with Gerald Smith, Huey Long's successor, their chances of victory in the coming election looked very good indeed.

Work section

A. Study cartoon A on the opposite page. Then, using the information you have read in this chapter as well as your own imagination, answer the following questions.
   1. On what famous event in ancient history is this cartoon based? Briefly tell the story of this event in your own words.
   2. Who do you think is meant to be inside the horse in this cartoon?
   3. Who is inside the fortress in this cartoon?
   4. What does the fortress gate represent? Which body of people kept it shut in 1935?
   5. What message do you think the cartoonist was trying to put across to the readers of the *Tribune*?

B. Study cartoon B on the opposite page, then answer these questions.
   1. Who is the man in the rowing boat? What does the rowing boat represent?
   2. Who do you think the man in the sea is meant to be?
   3. What did the Supreme Court say was an 'illegal act' in 1935?
   4. Explain what point you think the cartoonist was trying to make.
   5. Compare this cartoon with cartoon A. Do you think the cartoonist in each case was pro or anti the New Deal? Explain your answer.

C. What do you think Huey Long meant by 'Every man a king, but no man wears a crown'? Do you think this aim could have been achieved by his 'Share Our Wealth' movement? Explain your answer.

A SECOND NEW DEAL

As you have found out, Roosevelt's New Deal was running into serious problems in 1935. Extremists like Huey Long, Father Charles Coughlin and Doctor Frances Townsend were winning support. Trade unions were organising strikes. And the Supreme Court, in case after case, was declaring that Roosevelt had acted illegally in setting up the New Deal agencies.

Roosevelt's answer to these problems was to begin all over again. In 1935 he began a 'second New Deal' to replace the agencies that the Supreme Court had declared illegal.

The Wagner Act

The second New Deal began with an act concerning trade unions and industrial relations. The **National Labor Relations Act** was passed only six weeks after the Supreme Court killed the NRA by declaring its fair labour and fair wage codes illegal. This act, often called the **Wagner Act** after the Senator who thought it up, gave American workers the right to join and to form trade unions. It stopped employers from punishing workers who did so, and it set up a National Labor Relations Board to see that both employers and workers obeyed the act.

The Social Security Act

Next after the Wagner Act came the most important and lasting of all the New Deal laws, the **Social Security Act**. This act set up a national system of pensions for old people and widows. The payments were only $10 to a maximum of $85 monthly – a far cry from Doctor Townsend's demand for $200 a month – but at least it was a start. The act also provided help for the disabled and for children in need. Finally it set up a national system of unemployment insurance. This meant that anyone out of work would now receive financial help from

A roadside advertisement of 1936, part of a national advertising campaign to help get business out of the Depression

the government instead of having to rely on local charities.

To replace the Agricultural Adjustment Administration which the Supreme Court had declared illegal, Roosevelt now introduced the **Soil Conservation Act** in 1936. This allowed the government to give money to farmers if they conserved and improved the soil on their farms. It was an easy way for farmers to qualify for government money without breaking the Supreme Court's ruling.

The Presidential election of 1936

By November 1936, when elections for the Presidency were due to be held, Roosevelt's second New Deal was starting to work. So Roosevelt and the Democrats went into the election campaign feeling confident of a big victory. In his speeches Roosevelt used the slogan 'We have only just begun to fight', and he promised to continue the New Deal if he was re-elected.

The result was the greatest landslide victory in more than a century. All but two of the states voted Democrat. Twenty-seven million Americans cast their votes for Roosevelt, against sixteen million for Alf Landon, who was the Republican Party candidate.

Roosevelt now went forward for a second term of four years in the White House, believing that his greatest achievements were yet to come.

An American cartoon of the 1936 Presidential election. Only two states, Vermont and Maine, did not vote for Roosevelt in the election

Work section

A. Study the poster opposite.
1. Explain in your own words the message you think this poster is trying to put across.
2. Judging by what you have read in Part Two of this book, which groups in American society did *not* share in 'the world's highest standard of living'?
3. Which groups in American society do you think had gained a better standard of living as a result of the New Deal?

B. Suggest as many reasons as you can why President Roosevelt won a landslide victory in the Presidential elections of 1936.

C. Make revision notes on what you have read in Part Two of this book. There is a revision guide on the next page to help you.

23

Revision guide

These note-headings and sub-headings are designed to help you make notes for yourself on Part Two of this book. They are not a complete set of notes to be copied.

E. The New Deal and the unemployed
1. The CWA (Civil Works Administration)
   a) The ideas of Harry Hopkins
   b) The work of the CWA
   c) 'Boondoggling'
2. The PWA (Public Works Administration)
   a) The ideas of Harold Ickes
   b) The work of the PWA
3. The WPA (Works Progress Administration)
   a) The aim of the WPA
   b) The work of the WPA

F. The New Deal and the farmers
1. The problems of the farmers
2. The AAA (Agricultural Adjustment Administration)
3. The effects of AAA policies on sharecroppers
4. The Dust Bowl and its effects

G. The New Deal and the land
1. The CCC (Civilian Conservation Corps)
2. The TVA (Tennessee Valley Authority)

H. The New Deal and Industry
1. The problems of industry
2. The NRA (National Recovery Administration)
   a) The codes of the NRA
   b) The Blue Eagle
   c) The problems of the NRA

I. Opposition to the New Deal
1. The opposition of the Supreme Court
   a) The 'Sick Chickens' case, 1935
   b) Arguments about the constitution
2. Other ideas for a New Deal
   a) The 'Share Our Wealth' movement
   b) Father Charles Coughlin
   c) Doctor Frances Townsend

J. The second New Deal, 1935
1. The Wagner Act
2. The Social Security Act

Revision exercise

Roosevelt said in a speech in 1933 that the aim of the New Deal was 'relief, recovery and reform'. By 'relief' he meant helping the unemployed, the homeless and the hungry. By 'recovery' he meant getting America out of the Depression. By 'reform' he meant improving the American economy and American society.

Divide a page of your notebook into three columns. In each column write down the names of any act or agency of the New Deal that helped to bring relief, recovery or reform to America. To help you, all the acts and agencies of the New Deal are listed beneath.

In each case you should write a sentence explaining briefly how the agency helped.

Example:

Relief	Recovery	Reform
The CWA (Civil Works Administration). This agency provided relief by giving jobs to the unemployed on public work schemes.		

The Emergency Banking Act	(page 8)	The Agricultural Adjustment Administration	(page 14)
The Economy Act	(page 8)	The Civilian Conservation Corps	(page 16)
The Beer Act	(page 8)	The Tennessee Valley Authority	(page 17)
The Federal Emergency Relief Administration	(page 9)	The National Recovery Administration	(page 18)
Home Owners Loan Corporation	(page 9)	The National Labor Relations Act	(page 22)
The Civil Works Administration	(page 12)	The Social Security Act	(page 22)
The Public Works Administration	(page 12)	The Soil Conservation Act	(page 23)
The Works Progress Administration	(page 13)		

FROM NEW DEAL TO WORLD WAR

The 'Memorial Day Massacre' at the Republic Steel plant in Chicago, 31 May 1937

The photograph above was taken during a strike in 1937 by steel workers in Chicago. The steel workers of the Republic Steel Company were on strike because their employers would not let them join a trade union, even though the Wagner Act of 1936 (see page 22) gave all workers that right. On Memorial Day, a public holiday on 31 May, strikers were joined by their families for a protest march outside the steel plant.

As the marchers neared the plant 500 blue coated policemen formed a line barring their way. The chief of police ordered the marchers to turn back. When they refused he ordered the police to make a charge. Men, women and children suddenly retreated in panic as tear-gas grenades popped amongst them. Then the police drew their pistols and fired into the crowd.

At the end of the day nine of the marchers were dead, some with pistol shots in their backs, and more than a hundred were badly wounded. Veteran soldiers among the marchers said they saw more blood there than they had ever seen on a battlefield.

The Memorial Day Massacre was only one of many violent clashes between police and workers in the summer of 1937. Something seemed to be going wrong with the New Deal: the bad days of 1932–3, when talk of revolution was in the air, seemed to be returning. As Roosevelt began his second term of office Americans looked to him again for a solution to this new wave of troubles. Part Three shows how he tried but failed to provide a solution.

11

THE END OF THE NEW DEAL

A 'sit-down strike' in the General Motors plant in Michigan, January 1937. This method of striking was first used by rubber workers in Akron, Ohio, in 1935. By striking inside the factory, the workers prevented the management from using 'scab' labour to replace them

President Roosevelt began his second term of office in January 1937. In his inaugural speech he said:

'In this nation I see . . . millions of families trying to live on incomes so meagre that the pall [cloud] of family disaster hangs over them day by day.

I see millions whose daily lives in city and on farm continue under conditions labelled indecent by a so-called polite society half a century ago.

I see millions denied education, recreation, and the opportunity to better their lot and the lot of their children.

I see millions lacking the means to buy the products of farm and factory and by their poverty denying work and productiveness to many other millions.

I see one third of the nation ill-housed, ill-clad and ill-nourished.

It is not despair that I paint you in that picture. I paint it for you in hope – because the Nation proposes to paint it out.'

The problem of the Supreme Court

Before Roosevelt could 'paint out' the poverty, hunger and unemployment that still crippled America, he had to make sure that the Supreme Court would not continue to interfere in his work by declaring that his reforms were illegal.

The nine judges of the Supreme Court were all old. One was eighty, five were in their seventies and none was under sixty. Roosevelt put forward a new act, the **Judicial Reform Act**, saying that the Court was falling behind in its work because it had too much

26

work to do. The act gave Roosevelt the right to appoint six extra judges to help do the work. Although the act did not say so, Roosevelt would naturally appoint judges whom he knew agreed with him.

When the Supreme Court heard what was in store, they immediately stopped opposing Roosevelt. They did nothing to change the acts of the second New Deal – the Wagner Act, the Social Security Act and the Soil Conservation Act. Simply by threatening to appoint new judges who agreed with him, Roosevelt had succeeded in overcoming the opposition of the Supreme Court.

Roosevelt's threat to pack the Supreme Court with new judges was very unpopular. Many people accused him of wanting to rule America as a dictator. He became even more unpopular when a series of strikes and labour disputes broke out in 1937.

Strikes

The Wagner Act of 1935 gave American workers the right to join trade unions. In 1935 a new trade union, the **Congress of Industrial Organisation (CIO)**, was set up for unskilled workers in big industries such as cars and steel.

By 1937 the CIO had over three million members, but the managers of the biggest companies did not like it. They refused to allow their workers to join the CIO. They hired spies and special agents to find out who the unionists were. And they organised 'goon squads' of thugs and professional criminals to deal with unionists who made trouble for the management.

In 1937 workers in the car and steel industries went on strike. Some of these strikes were 'sit-down' strikes in which the workers occupied the factories to prevent any work from being done. Others were all-out strikes, often involving violent clashes with police and 'goon squads' who tried to break up their picket lines.

The strikes succeeded. Under pressure from the government, the managers allowed the workers to use their legal right to join the CIO. But the violence and disruption involved in the strikes added to Roosevelt's unpopularity in 1937.

A new depression

During 1937 Roosevelt cut back the amount of money the federal government was spending. He did not want America to get into debt, and he believed that the state governments were able to deal with the problems of the Depression without more help from the federal government.

Unfortunately this cut in spending came at the same time as a decline in world trade. Unemployment suddenly shot up to 10.5 million in 1938. Steel and car production fell. Share prices on the stock exchange plunged.

Roosevelt's problems were made worse when elections for Congress were held in 1938. The Republican Party won a majority of seats, and this meant that Roosevelt now found it hard to persuade Congress to pass the laws he wanted. As a result Roosevelt did not introduce any new laws to combat the Depression. Unemployment therefore remained very high for the next two years.

In 1940 Presidential elections were held again. This time it seemed less certain that Roosevelt would win. After a brilliant election campaign, however, Roosevelt beat his Republican opponent by five million votes, becoming the first American President to serve three consecutive terms in office.

Work section

A. Study the extract from Roosevelt's inaugural speech on the opposite page, then answer the following questions:
  1. List six ways in which Roosevelt thought that conditions were still bad in America.
  2. Why do you think so many Americans were still living in bad conditions after four years of the New Deal? Explain your answer.

B. Study the photograph opposite of a sit-down strike.
  1. Which New Deal law allowed workers like these to join a trade union?
  2. Why do you think many bosses of car-making and steel plants did not want their workers to join trade unions?
  3. Compare this photograph with the photograph of the 'Memorial Day Massacre' on page 25. Judging by what you have read, why do you think there was so much violence involved in the strikes of 1937?

C. In the Presidential election of 1940 these slogans were used by the Democratic and Republican parties:
  'No man is good three times.'
  'Better a third-termer than a third rater.'
  1. Which do you think was the Democratic slogan, and which was the Republican? Give reasons for your answer.
  2. Explain in your own words what you think each slogan meant.

12

AMERICA AND THE SECOND WORLD WAR

Until 1939 Roosevelt and the American government kept out of the affairs of other countries. Between 1935 and 1937 Congress passed a series of **neutrality laws** to keep America out of wars overseas. They stated that Americans must not trade with or give financial help to any country at war.

The Cash and Carry Plan

In September 1939 the Second World War began. In Europe, Britain and France got ready to fight Germany. Roosevelt feared that if Germany defeated France and Britain, then other countries, including America, might come under attack. He therefore asked Congress to change the neutrality laws so that America could give help to Britain and France. In November 1939 Congress agreed to a new scheme called the **Cash and Carry Plan**. By this plan Britain and France could buy goods and weapons from America if they collected them in their own ships.

The Cash and Carry Plan was no help to France. Less than a year later, in June 1940, German armies attacked and defeated France. At the same time they defeated a large British army at Dunkirk.

Britain now had to fight alone. America provided Britain with every weapon she possibly could, and in September 1940 gave her fifty destroyers to protect the ships carrying supplies across the Atlantic. Before long, however, Britain had run short cash and could no longer buy all the weapons she needed on the cash and carry basis.

Lend-Lease

In place of the Cash and Carry Plan, Roosevelt drew up a **Lend-Lease Bill**. This would allow America to

Two of the fifty destroyers that America gave Britain in 1940

B-24 bombers on the assembly line in Detroit, Michigan, November 1943

lend military equipment to Britain free of charge. There were big public demonstrations against the bill. Organisations such as the 'Mothers' Crusade' and the 'America First Committee' wanted Roosevelt to keep America out of the war between Britain and Germany. But Congress passed the bill in March 1941. Vast amounts of American equipment were soon crossing the Atlantic and pouring in to Britain. Later in 1941, when Germany invaded Russia, America also sent great amounts of equipment to the Russians under the Lend-Lease Act.

In August 1941 Roosevelt met the British Prime Minister, Winston Churchill, for a series of talks. The talks were held at sea on board USS *Augusta*, an American cruiser. There they signed the **Atlantic Charter**, agreeing to work together for international peace after the war was finished.

Pearl Harbour

Meanwhile, on the other side of the world, the Japanese armed forces were invading Japan's neighbours. By 1941 China had been attacked and occupied, and French Indo-China was under attack. In protest, Roosevelt banned exports of oil and steel to Japan. Relations between Japan and America grew cold.

On 7 December 1941 Japanese dive bombers and torpedo bombers attacked the American fleet in its base at **Pearl Harbour** in the Pacific Ocean. In the attack they sank eight battleships and killed more than 2000 sailors. The next day America declared war on Japan. Three days after that, Japan's allies, Italy and Germany, declared war on America.

America at war

For the next four years, 1941 to 1945, American soldiers, sailors and airmen fought in Europe, North Africa and the Pacific. In all, 7.2 million American servicemen fought in the Second World War.

To keep this enormous army supplied with weapons and equipment, American industry had to boost its output massively. New factories were built and old ones were converted to make the machinery of war. People who had been unemployed throughout the Depression now found it easy to get work.

By 1945 the American government was spending $100 billion a year on fighting in the Second World War, and unemployment had dropped to under one million.

The 'Big Three' at the Yalta Conference in 1945: Winston Churchill (left), Franklin D. Roosevelt (centre), and Joseph Stalin (right)

The end of the war

In November 1944 Roosevelt stood for election as President for a fourth term of office. For a fourth time he won the Presidential election.

By this time the Allied armies of Britain, America and Russia were winning the war against Germany and Japan.

Three days after taking the oath of office in January 1945, Roosevelt left America to travel to Russia for a meeting with Winston Churchill and Joseph Stalin, leader of Russia. The meeting was held at Yalta on the Black Sea. The three Allied leaders made many important decisions at the **Yalta Conference** – about the future of Germany after the war was over, about how to win the war against Japan, and about a new world peace-keeping organisation, the **United Nations**. This last one was an important decision for the future of America. By agreeing to join the United Nations Organisation, Roosevelt made sure that America would no longer keep out of the affairs of the world as she had done in the 1920s and 1930s.

Shortly after returning to America from Yalta, Roosevelt took a holiday. On the morning of 12 April 1945, while sitting by the fire reading, he suddenly suffered a stroke and lost consciousness. Four hours later he died.

Roosevelt was succeeded by the Vice President, Harry Truman. Only three weeks later Germany surrendered to the Allies.

Work section

A. What does neutrality mean? In what way was America a neutral country during the 1930s?

B. Explain how America gradually ended her neutrality on each of the following dates: November 1939, September 1940, March 1941, August 1941, December 1941.

C. During the Second World War unemployment in America dropped from over nine million to less than one million. Suggest two reasons why unemployment fell so much during the war.

13

ASSESSING ROOSEVELT AND THE NEW DEAL

Since the United States of America was founded in 1776 there have been forty Presidents. Many Americans today regard Franklin Roosevelt, the 32nd President, as one of the greatest. This chapter invites you to decide whether you agree with this judgement, and to make your own assessment of Roosevelt and the New Deal. Let us begin by finding out what people living at the time of the New Deal thought about him.

Contemporary opinions

Americans felt strongly about Roosevelt. They either loved him or they hated him, as these sources show.

A. This joke about the New Deal appeared on the back of a businessman's calling card:

'Four thousand years ago Moses said to his people: "Pick up your shovels, mount your asses, load your camels, and ride to the promised land".

Four thousand years later Mr Roosevelt said to HIS people: "Throw down your shovels, sit on your asses, light up a Camel [*a brand of American cigarette*] THIS is the promised land".'

B. This comes from *Harper's Magazine* 1935:

'As a social and economic class we, who have lived or tried to live in any part on money saved, are being liquidated.'

C. These imaginary figures had the title of *Confidential report of Conditions of the Nation Under the New Deal*:

'Population of the United States   124,000,000
Eligible for Old Age Pensions   30,000,000
That leaves to do the work   94,000,000
Persons working for the
    government   20,000,000
That leaves to do the work   74,000,000
Ineligible to work under the
    Child Labor Law   60,000,000
That leaves to do the work   14,000,000
Number unemployed in the
    Nation   13,999,998
That leaves to do the work   2
ME AND THE PRESIDENT.
HE HAS GONE FISHING
AND I AM GETTING DAMN TIRED.'

D. *'Yes, you remembered me.' A cartoon of 1933*

E. This is from an article in *Time Magazine*, April 1936:

'Regardless of party and regardless of region, today, with few exceptions, members of the so-called Upper Class frankly hate Franklin Roosevelt.'

F. This was an anonymous duet to be sung by Franklin Roosevelt and his wife Eleanor.

'You kiss the Negroes,
I'll kiss the Jews,
We'll stay in the White House
As long as we choose.'

G. Another popular verse in 1937 put these words into Roosevelt's mouth:

'When the organisers needed dough
I closed up the plants for the CIO.
I ruined jobs and I ruined health,
And I put the screws on the rich man's wealth.'

H. Other Americans wrote directly to Roosevelt. This is a letter sent to the White House, 1934.

'Dear Mr President,

This is just to tell you everything is all right now. The man you sent found our house all right and we went down the bank with him and the mortgage can go a while longer. You remember I wrote you about losing the furniture too. Well, your man got it back for us. I never heard of a President like you, Mr Roosevelt. Mrs _____ and I are old folks and don't amount to much, but we are joined with those millions of others in praying for you every night. God bless you, Mr Roosevelt.'

I. And two envelopes of letters sent to Roosevelt had these addresses:

'God's Gift to the USA,
The White House.'

'To the Greatest Man in the World,
The White House.'

The opinions of historians

Historians have written many books about Roosevelt and the New Deal. Here are the judgements of three American historians, William Leuchtenburg, Arthur M. Schlesinger, and Joseph Alsop.

J. 'The New Deal certainly did not get the country out of the Depression. As late as 1941 there were still six million unemployed and it was really not until the war that the army of the jobless finally disappeared.'

K. 'The recovery programme of 1933 made no basic changes in the American economy. In its frenzied way it started the wheels of industry turning again; . . . it raised agricultural prices.

The business situation achieved a measure of stability, and basic social rights won a measure of government guarantee.'

L. 'I do not believe that the real essence of Roosevelt's achievement on the home front is to be found in the list of new federal agencies he created. . . . Instead, the very essence of his achievement . . . derived from the combined impact of all his domestic reforms. On a very wide front and in the truest possible sense, Franklin Delano Roosevelt included the excluded.'

Some statistics

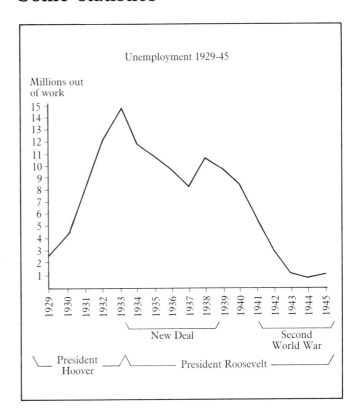

Unemployment 1929-45

Work section

A. Study sources A to I, then answer these questions.
1. Identify by letter which of these sources is pro-Roosevelt and which is anti-Roosevelt.
2. Study the anti-Roosevelt sources you have identified. According to these sources, what kind of people disliked Roosevelt and the New Deal? Suggest as many reasons as you can why these people disliked the New Deal.
3. According to the pro-Roosevelt sources you have identified, what kinds of people liked Roosevelt and the New Deal? For what reasons did such people support the New Deal?

B. Study sources J to L above, then answer these questions.
1. Compare source I with the graph showing unemployment 1929 to 1945. Do you think the judgement made by this historian is a fair one? Explain your answer with reference to figures taken from the graph.
2. In source L, what do you think the historian meant by 'Franklin Delano Roosevelt included the excluded'?

C. Make revision notes on what you have read in Part Three of this book. There is a revision guide on the next page to help you.

Revision guide

These note headings and sub-headings are intended as a framework for notes which you make for yourself. They are not a complete set of notes to be copied. They follow on from the notes you have already made.

K. The end of the New Deal
1. How Roosevelt overcame the problem of the Supreme Court
2. The strikes of 1937
3. The Depression of 1937–8
4. The elections for Congress in 1938

L. America and the Second World War
1. American neutrality

2. How American neutrality came to an end
   a) The Cash and Carry Plan
   b) The Lend-Lease Act
   c) The Atlantic Charter
   d) Pearl Harbour
3. The effects of the war on America
4. The Yalta Conference

Revision exercise

What is your opinion of the New Deal? Was it a success or a failure? Try doing this exercise to help you make up your mind.

In column A there are six opinions about various aspects of the New Deal. In column B there are six pieces of evidence that agree with these opinions. In column C there are five pieces of evidence that disagree with the opinions. All the opinions and pieces of evidence are jumbled up.
1. Sort out the statements in columns B and C which go with the opinions in column A.
2. Link them together with words of your own. For example: 'The New Deal did not solve the problem of unemployment. Unemployment never dropped below six million during the 1930s. On the other hand, the New Deal provided jobs for many millions of people even though it did not give jobs to all the unemployed.'
3. Use the linked sentences to write an essay in answer to the question 'Was the New Deal a success or a failure?'

Column A	Column B	Column C
The New Deal did not solve the problems of homelessness, poverty and hunger.	Unemployment never dropped below six million during the 1930s.	The New Deal provided jobs for many millions of people, even though it did not provide jobs for all the unemployed.
The New Deal helped the farmers in the countryside.	Over half the trees in America today were planted during the New Deal. The problem of the Dustbowl has been overcome. The TVA is still in existence, controlling the Tennessee River.	Many employers ignored the Wagner Act and refused to let their workers join trade unions.
The New Deal helped workers in industry by giving them the right to join trade unions.	All Americans over the age of sixty received pensions of between $10 and $85 per month.	Sharecroppers continued to live in terrible poverty. The New Deal did nothing for the 'Okies' and 'Arkies' escaping from the Dustbowl.
The New Deal did not solve the problem of unemployment.	Roosevelt admitted in 1937 that one third of all Americans were ill-housed, ill-clad and badly nourished.	Old age pensions were much lower than Doctor Townsend and the Pensions League demanded.
The New Deal improved the land enormously.	The Wagner Act of 1935 set up the National Labor Relations Board to protect workers.	The Home Owners Loan Corporation helped millions of home-owners to avoid eviction by lending them money to pay their mortgages. There were no Hoovervilles left by 1939.
The New Deal gave Americans social security for the first time in their history.	The AAA increased crop prices and this pushed up farmers' profits.	